It's Okay to be Alone

*A hands-on guide to coping with
canine separation anxiety*

Julie Hindle

It's Okay to be Alone

Published by Abelenus Press
First published on Kindle 2015. Revised 2017
First Edition Paperback 2017

Photo credits:
Cover photograph (Cover Girl Amara) © 2015 Julie Hindle
All photographs © Julie Hindle, except for
© Krista Guziolek - pages 14, 87 and 90
© Nicolette Tracey - page 68
© Jamie Hindle – page 16
© Abby Webb – page 77

Table of Contents

01 Why I Wrote this Book

Separation Anxiety is one of the most common canine behavioural disorders at this time. It leads to many dogs ending up in rescue centres or even being euthanised.

However, the good news is, it is also highly treatable.

I wrote this book in memory of all the owners of dogs that I have helped overcome this anxiety, for all the dogs that have been misdiagnosed and labelled as having this condition when they are simply misunderstood, but most of all I wrote this book for all the dogs yet to come, that they may never have to suffer separation anxiety, if only their owners would read and learn to understand their dogs needs and know that they are not born with this condition, that it is not about the breed they are, or their temperament, their stubbornness or dominance.

Separation Anxiety is something that any dog may develop because something has gone wrong in their training, or a bad experience happens to freak them out when they were left home alone. This is then compounded by the fact that the new owner doesn't know how to prevent or handle the situation when they first exhibit the anxiety. If this book prevents one such case then it has achieved its goal.

From the time, I first published this book, two years ago on Kindle, the feed-back from it has been so amazing and has led to many owners contacting me and telling the difference it has made understanding that this behaviour was completely avoidable and that their dogs no longer need to suffer. I decided to revise and put this book into paper back format due to the demand from many dog owners.

Because I will be using the term 'separation anxiety' a lot throughout the book I will use the abbreviation 'SA', through the body of the text for ease of reading.

What I hope you will gain from this book

If you have a dog suffering with SA, this book will give you the hands-on tools you need to understand and cope with it, by giving you a step-by-step guide to solving or preventing your dog from ever being stressed when left alone.

If you are thinking of getting a puppy, or a rescue dog, this book will prevent the problem from starting, if you follow the methods from beginning to end, forewarned is forearmed.

I learnt a long time ago that being a 'dog trainer' is not only about teaching the dog, but is mostly about teaching the person to teach their dog. In this hands-on guide, it is my task to teach you, and it is your task to teach your dog to overcome any SA issues that he or she might have.

The methods given in this book are based on my experience over almost 30 years as an Applied Canine Behaviourist and Dog Trainer. It is worth remembering that, not every method works for every dog and not every case of SA is that simple to solve. Extreme cases of SA may require the assistance of a Behaviourist to visit with you and your dog.

If you are in any doubt about your dog's behaviour, please contact your veterinarian for further advice and guidance to a Behaviourist they recommend.

Please read this book in its entirety, every step and page is important to understanding, treating and preventing separation anxiety. If you are reading this book but don't actually have a dog with this problem or you are considering getting a dog, it is great you are being pro-active in avoiding problems for the future, the information found here will provide you with the right steps to prevent SA from developing.

02 What is Separation Anxiety?

SA is not gender specific, neither is it breed specific. Any dog can develop it at any time. For ease of reading I will refer to the dog as she throughout this book, unless the context is gender specific.

SA is a stress disorder which escalates, often due to changes in a dog's circumstances. It can often, develop without the owner noticing, until their seemingly well-balanced dog has grown from a puppy to a young adult dog, having been allowed to go about her own business at home. Around a year to eighteen months (if it hasn't happened before), the dog may appear to develop a problem being left alone.

The anxiety a dog displays can vary from a minor issue to a serious problem. Separation anxiety is in the top three most common problems I am called to deal with, although the degree of anxiety may vary enormously.

Understanding SA

True separation anxiety is quite heart rending, it can be very distressing, and is very sad to watch a dog who exhibits this. It can cause major problems for a family going through this.

One of two main emotions triggers Separation Anxiety, fear and frustration. Fear of being alone – the dog is fearful that something bad might happen, or the owner won't return, or the frustration of being left alone, because the dog wants their family back together and because things are not the way they think they should be.

Separation Anxiety is often incorrectly labelled. However, the problem is a big one and has been for years. It is also steadily growing, becoming more and more common amongst pet dogs. This is most likely due to the fact that more people need to go to work and their dogs spend more time home alone, without being taught that being alone is find. With the right training and upbringing from puppyhood, going out need and leaving your dog at home, never become a problem for your dog.

The problem of separation anxiety is so great that in 2014 there was a television documentary showing us how stressed our canine friends become when we leave them home alone. It was a bit of a generalisation, as not all dogs walk the floor boards or cry hysterically then they are left home alone.

It is okay for your dog to be alone some of the time and not all dogs that are left home alone exhibit stress behaviours, your role is to provide security and stability so that your dog does not feel fearful or anxious and is capable of relaxing in her own company.

03 Understanding your Dog

In this chapter

- It's just a sound
- They have needs too
- A friend and a companion
- You can't pretend to be a dog
- Laying firm foundations
- Shelve your emotions

I love that we love our dogs as much as we do, but it would be so much better for dogs if we showed our love in the way that is best for the dog, not for us. Dogs need food, water, exercise, structure, rules, boundaries, daylight, sleep, play, affection. What they don't need is clothes; make up, hair dyes, accessories, silk to sleep on, or a four-poster bed.

It would be great if when you decide to own a dog that you showed your love for them by learning to understand them first, before expecting them to understand you. It is your responsibility to learn what your dog is saying to you. This will halve any problem you think you have, once you have achieved the balance of what your dog needs, then by all means you can start showering her with the other elements, although a little discretion might be wise.

It's just a sound

Put yourselves in their shoes, (if they had any), for just a moment.

Imagine going to live in a house where no one speaks the same language as you, they keep telling you to do something and keep pushing you from place to place. They keep making noises at you and don't seem very relaxed in your company. You can hear their sound, but you don't know what any of it means.

Imagine how confused and frustrating that would be for you. How unnerving it would be, not knowing if you were getting it right or wrong, not knowing if you belong because of their unpredictable behaviour towards you. This is how I think a dog must feel and it's no wonder that some dogs start to display aggression at the approach of the owner.

Take time out to watch, read and learn about the wonderful animal you have chosen to share your life with. Stop assuming they understand you and that they know what is right and wrong, how can they if they have never been taught, it is a 'dog'. Taking time to understand your dog will go a long way to help you in developing a strong bond together. You cannot correct a dog for doing something you consider wrong, if she has never been taught what is right.

Teach them, they need to know where they fit in and what is expected of them, help them to understand 'you', by being their teacher and by being a consistent team leader. Aggression and bullying should have no place in raising your dog.

Dogs have needs too

It is our job to meet our dog's needs at all times. Therefore we must work to teach our dogs that we will return to them and that it is ok to be left home alone. That you make the decisions and have the right to leave the den when you choose, without them following you, just as a pup would do when the pack go off to hunt, they are left behind in the den. If your dog is confident in you as their leader, you have taught them well and they trust you, they will relax when you are gone and await your return. Helping them to see you departing as a positive and not a negative is essential, it will all become clear as you read on.

A Friend and a Companion

For years we have been taught that dogs are a 'pack animal' and when they live as part of a pack their world is built upon structure and rules and working as part of a team. What we now also know is that dogs are incredibly flexible and adaptable, they can adapt too many environments and conditions, they have evolved and are now a domesticated animal, and they are our pets. It is this time over centuries, that has given us the dog we know today and it is because of how they have evolved that they are the

world's most popular pet. At a rough estimate there are at least 525 million dogs on the planet.

They are not wolves, they are dogs. Whilst our dogs have descended from the wolf, they are very different in how they develop mentally to their distant cousins. For example, did you know that a wolf can never be tamed? No matter how much human interaction they receive and no matter how much training they receive, the will revert to their wild instincts when they are approaching maturity.

It is said the dog as we know it, never really develops beyond what would be the juvenile state of their wild ancestor the wolf. They remain in a kind a pup like mode, throughout their lives, due to domestication, which is why they live so happily alongside us and are happy to take instruction and guidance from us.

You can't pretend to be a dog

You can't kid a dog, your dog knows that you are not a dog and you don't need to pretend to be one, but it would help them enormously if you understood their language. They do

still need leadership, but the right kind of leadership in order that you can both benefit from each other.

It is a two-way street, she is your friend and your companion but you should also be her friend and her companion. There are good leaders and bad leaders; you do not need to be a dominating leader for your dog to understand how to live with you and what it is you want, so right now you can put down the dog bowl and stop pretending to eat before her, it is not needed.

I remember many years ago going to a training school with my dog and the head trainer addressing the class explained. 'You must not smile at your dog, because they think you are showing your teeth at them as they do to one another and they could see this as a threat', Hmmm. I am not even going to comment on this statement, except to say, please keep smiling at your dog, they learn to identify with it and relax in your happiness.

Laying firm foundations

The correct foundation being laid for your dog is essential if you are to prevent anxiety from developing. Good solid foundation training forms the basic building blocks upon which all future training is built. As I said earlier, it is my opinion that most dogs who stress when you leave the room or the house do so because of you, the owner and how you live with your dog. This may come across as blunt but it is the fact of the matter and my job in this book is to help you see this and, more importantly help you to put it right.

Shelve your emotions

Emotions can get in the way when you feel sorry for your dog; they can prevent you from carrying out the necessary training of teaching the dog to feel comfortable in their own environment. This is one of the main causes that I believe leads to separation anxiety.

04 What makes a Dog a Dog?

In this chapter
- What we do + How we live = A specific result
- Which dogs are prone to separation anxiety?
- Prevention is better than cure

It may not seem natural for the dog, whose ancestors were pack animals, to be left home alone. Remember also that as a pack animal they would have originally been a traveller. Sometimes travelling hundreds of miles in a day to find food, they were not an animal who resided at home all day. However that was then and this is now, they have evolved over thousands of years to adapt to the environment and life they are faced with.

As I said at the beginning of this book, dogs are adaptable. They can live in isolation as a stray, without ever becoming part of a pack. They can live in apartments, in a house, in the country, in a kennel, on a boat, they can live as a single dog, in a home with humans, and they can live with other dogs, with many other pets and with children. They don't need to hunt and kill to survive, they can survive equally well as a scavenger, and they are the most versatile of all creatures.

Given how adaptive they are to their environment, it should come as no great surprise that they can learn to live alone for a few hours a day, without going into a depressed state. Not all dogs pace up and down when we leave them, salivate and drool, bark and whine and wreck the house, despite what some 'experts' would have us believe.

What we do + How we live = A specific result

One thing I have learnt over my years as a canine behaviourist is that dogs are consistent. What we do with them and how we live with them produces a specific result. For me this has never changed. There is no doubt that we all have seen or experienced how clever or intelligent dogs can be, however they are also a creature of habit and they learn by repetition, the good and the not so good, what's pleasant and what is not.

Being a creature of habit, means it doesn't take long for your dog to become conditioned to respond in a particular way. Behaviourally, dogs don't change how they think, how they socialise, how they relate to people and to their own kind. However, add people into their equation and we can and do cause dogs to sometimes behave in seemingly strange and neurotic ways.

Dogs thrive on rules, boundaries and structure; lack of these three ingredients, causes problems for our dogs, namely frustration and at times insecurity. If you follow a set structure in raising a puppy, or introducing a dog into your home, most of the 'behavioural problems' people experience with them would be avoided. As with most things in life and dog training is no exception, it is ever changing and developing, mostly for the good and betterment of dogs. The minute we mention the words rules, boundaries and structure it conjures up the image of domination for many, it does not have to mean this. Children need rules, boundaries and structure if they are to grow into a responsible citizen, or so we hope. Dogs are no different they cannot be left to get on and do their own thing or things start to go seriously wrong within the home.

Which dogs are prone to separation anxiety?

Over the 30 years that I have worked with dogs, I have answered the desperate call, on many occasions from owners desperate to know why their dogs howl, bark, wee, poo, and destroy the home when the owner dares to leave them alone in their home.

The reason why some dogs and not others suffer from separation anxiety isn't always clear. Is it a trauma somewhere in the dog's development that triggers it? Is it just down to individual personalities? In my opinion, individual personalities may have a big part to play in it, what one dog copes with, another dog may not.

I often read people's problems when shared on public media such as face book etc. they explain the problems they are having and proceed to ask for help. They often get many replies which can sometimes be quite overwhelming. More often than not, there is that one reply,

"My dog has never had a problem and I do it this way".

This is immaterial, because different dogs will react differently, to how much freedom they are given. Different people and families, live differently with their dogs so they will get a different reaction.

Prevention is better than cure

What is impossible to tell is how 'your' dog is going to react to the freedom given, so taking some precautions from the beginning, can prevent separation anxiety from ever developing. 'Prevention is better than cure'. There is no point waiting to see if something happens and then trying to solve it, when you could have prevented it in the first place.

The cause of separation anxiety 'through frustration', is I believe caused primarily by how we live with our dog on a day-to-day basis. It is caused by how we live with our puppy from the day we bring her home, and what expectations we put on our puppy, or not as the case may be.

This will determine how our puppy deals with the situations she is faced with, in this case being left home alone. It can often develop very quickly with dogs that have come from rescue homes to become part of a family, because of how they are introduced into the home environment.

See section/s *How to prevent your new puppy from developing separation anxiety* and *How to prevent your rescue dog from developing separation anxiety.*

There is no doubt that some dogs not only object to their owner leaving them, but will also exhibit extreme stress when this happens. Worst-case scenario, some dogs can be so stressed at being left that they will cause severe damage to the owner's property and in turn may cause damage to themselves, some dogs have even been known to self-mutilate due to the high levels of stress they are experiencing and their determination to relieve the feeling. It is common for a noise pollution order to be levied on you and your family if a neighbour complains about the noise, even the best neighbour, will only tolerate so much of a crying or howling dog.

Every owner I have ever met has an ideal image of their puppy, living in harmony alongside their children, happily sitting alongside the family wherever they are in the home, wandering around the home, being the guardian, keeping watch over the family and home whether the family are out or in bed. There is nothing wrong with wanting this ideal, but you need to follow a procedure to get there, in order to prevent problems arising along the way.

05 Recognising Separation Anxiety

In this chapter
- Separation Anxiety through fear
- Identifying fear anxiety
- A Successful SA story – Barney Boxer

A dog may display separation anxiety in various ways when left alone, for example: Howling, barking, and whining – it may be one, two or a combination of all three of these. Toileting indoors – weeing, pooing or both. In the worst case scenario, Shivering and shaking, excessive panting and drooling pools of saliva. Destruction – chewing doors, windows, flooring and even self- mutilation.

Important Note: You must be careful not to confuse your dogs' desire to chew through boredom or just because it can, with that of SA.

When a dog is destroying the home, due to separation anxiety they will often target exit areas,

- Windows, doors, flooring. These are all means of escape and potential entry to the outside world.

- Chewing also releases endorphins in the brain which helps relieve stress, frustration and can also relieve pain.

- Whining and pacing up and down, possibly in circles, before and after you leave.

- The pads of their feet may be sweaty.

The symptoms a dog exhibits are determined by whether the anxiety is driven by one of two emotions, fear or frustration.

Separation Anxiety through fear

All separation anxiety is hard to watch, but separation anxiety caused through fear, is so difficult to go through, for both dog and owner. It is much harder to know, what it is that has triggered this type of anxiety.

It can often develop through something that has happened when the owner isn't present. This makes it even more difficult for the owner to pinpoint.

- A bad experience when left home alone is enough to trigger this.

- It could be a loud noise that has gone off or something that has fallen and frightened the dog.

- It could be a burglary.

- It may also be that the dog has always been sensitive and insecure and the owner has always offered security and protection by keeping her close to her, creating dependency.

Identifying fear-based anxiety

A dog exhibiting separation anxiety based through fear, may show one or a combination of the following behaviours.

- Shivering and shaking, excessive panting & drooling - many dogs will pant through stress and overheat.

- Whining and pacing—this may continue for hours.

- A dog's fear can be so extreme that they hyperventilates, leaving pools of saliva everywhere they go.

- Reluctance to eat - many dogs are social eaters and like the company of their pack around them in order to relax into eating.

- Toileting- Some dogs when stressed, will lose control of their bladder or bowel. However, many are simply stimulated to toilet due to the amount of moving around they do.

- Destruction of the home - The dog's determination to get out of the house is so great, she may try to break through doors, windows and even chew through walls. As a result she may not even register if she is causing damage to herself.

- The destruction the dog may cause will usually be at exits and entrances. I.e. window ledges, door frames, carpet by the doors because this is their potential entry to the outside world.

- Sometimes they may try climbing as high as possible, in the hope to find a way out if all else is failing.

The anxiety can be so great and so intense for some dogs their attempts to escape may even lead them to attempt, crashing through windows and doors, as in the case of Barney's story.

A Successful SA story - Barney Boxer

Some years ago a client had received a phone call to her work demanding that she return home immediately, her Boxer dog had smashed through a top floor window, landing on the street below. As a result he had lost half his nose, cut his head and eye open pretty badly and had broken his shoulder bone. He had also gone into severe shock and wouldn't let anyone near him, display aggression through fear and pain.

This incident was caused through fear based separation anxiety. This dog was eventually cured of his problems but his owner had to take some leave from work in order to succeed in helping him overcome his problems. Slowly over time, following a very strict routine of confidence building exercises Barney became a well-balanced dog.

Dogs with this degree of SA are highly stressed and unpredictable. If your dog is this extreme, you should definitely seek professional help to aid you in helping your dog, through the fear that he is showing you. If you feel confident enough that you would like to have ago using the methods in this book, go for it, but if you are not achieving some calm for your dog within a couple of weeks, then please seek help.

06 Letting go = Moving forward

In this chapter

It is important that fear is handled sensitively and calmly. What triggered the behaviour is irrelevant to trying to solve the problem for your dog. So let it go, as frustrating as it is that you may not know what caused it, hanging onto it could prevent and delay you helping your dog overcome the anxiety

Fear based separation anxiety is often difficult to pinpoint, although there is always the exception to the rule. It is often difficult with extreme separation anxiety, which is fear based, to pinpoint what caused it in the first place.

Just because your dog may suffer from separation anxiety, doesn't necessarily mean your dog has a deep-seated psychological problem, which is going to take forever and cost a fortune to solve. In fact as I said earlier, separation anxiety is a very treatable condition and shouldn't take long to correct if you follow a set method and set your emotions aside.

Depending on the scale of the problem we are dealing with, you may see results within 1 or 2 weeks, with a serious case of fear related SA, this may take 6 to 8 weeks.

Remain consistent and you will soon have a relaxed, confident dog that accepts you going about your business and who no longer stresses. If you are not consistent, you will have a confused dog that is unsure what you expect of her and is unsure of you as her leader, as good leaders are never unpredictable.

Separation Anxiety through frustration

Often seen in dogs who are allowed to go wherever they like in the house. They wander around all day while you are home, following you around wherever you go, in and out of the garden when it suits them. This creates a dependency or even a false sense of you and her must remain together at all times. Your dog may feel she has the right to be with you at all times and leaving her at home creates a big problem for her.

Identifying Separation Anxiety through frustration

- Barking, whining, and howling – even if you move to another room in the home, unless she is allowed to follow you.
- They may also wee or poo
- Destroy anything they can get their little paws on.
- Dig, pant and hyperventilate.
- She is allowed to follow you from room to room when you are at home.
- She waits outside the toilet door for you.

- She may even accompany you when you have a bath.

- She may sleep in your bedroom at night.

As mentioned earlier, this type of upbringing leads a dog into a false sense of where they fit in within the home. Many of the problems I see could have been avoided if this open plan arrangement was not in place.

Giving your dog *carte blanche* to go where she wants, you are pretty much giving her the keys to the castle and telling her it's all hers to do what she wants with. In response to this she is very likely to begin objecting to you leaving without her.

You have caused confusion for her; it is wrong to give her complete freedom and then when it suits you take it back, which is exactly what you are doing if you recognise this arrangement. Dogs are consistent and thrive on continuity, hap hazard arrangements cause confusion which in turn causes the frustration and her way of showing her frustration is to object to being left behind.

This balance needs addressing or many other issues can develop from this behaviour. The following exercise will re-address your dogs' mental well-being and how she sees things, putting you and your family back into the driving seat, helping your dog become a participating family member rather than a controlling family member.

07 Assessing and Diagnosing Separation Anxiety

In this chapter
- Assess your dog questionnaire
- Set 1 – Questions to assess how much freedom your dog has around the home
- Set 2 – Questions to assess your dogs' use of the crate/den

Attending behavioural home visits were separation anxiety is apparent, I ask the question, "How much freedom in the home is your dog allowed to have?" With a real sense of pride many tell me, "She can wander anywhere she wants in the home". As though restricting her would be a denial of her rights. Then there are those who like to point out to me, that they have some control of the dog, by saying, "Of course she's not allowed up-stairs". Blocking upstairs is not enough for her to understand her place within the family.

Of course this image I describe of your dog wandering free in your home can always be a possible long-term plan, but definitely not until your dog learns the rules and boundaries. Just as with children, every youngster must know there are rules and boundaries, right? Particularly if you are to get along and know where you all stand.

Even when you eventually give freedom to your dog, there must still be restrictions so that your dog knows, the home is yours and she gets to share it with you. You determine what access she can have and when she can have it, to certain areas. You should determine where and when she gets to wander. Establishing this element of leadership will make for a much happier home for you both. Your dog is a valued member of your family but you must help her to understand where she fits in if separation anxiety is to be avoided. This is achieved by establishing the rules, boundaries and guidelines with her from the moment she enters your world. There should be no grey or blurred areas.

Assess your dog – Questionnaire

The following is a series questions designed to help you recognize, assess and diagnose what is going on with your dog. It is my hope that in answering these questions, they will help you think about, what it is that is bothering your dog. Helping you ask the right questions that you hadn't otherwise thought about. Please don't omit these questions, as they hold the key in helping you better understand separation anxiety in 'your' dog.

Understanding and learning how to diagnose what your dog is going through, puts you one step closer to solving the problem.

The questions will

- Help you think through what your dog is doing and why.
- Recognise whether your dog has separation anxiety through fear, frustration or perhaps a mixture of both, or even help you decide whether she has true separation anxiety at all.

Answer the questions honestly and thoroughly, some of the answers will be very obvious to you; for others you may need to watch your dog over the course of a day or two to be clear about your answer.

Use a notebook and pen and write your dog's reactions down throughout the period of a day and evening.

If you are uncertain how your dog reacts when she is left home alone, now may be a good time to set a camera up, so that you can record one of your sessions away from home.

These 2 sets of questions will allow you to make an informed decision on answering the questions.

Set 1

Assess if your dog has too much freedom

Q1. Does your dog follow you from room to room at home?   YES or NO

Hopefully your answer is No, but if your answer is Yes - then in following you around, your dog is able to keep tabs on where you go. This sets up in her mind that you cannot go anywhere without her knowing about it, because you have allowed this to happen.

You may believe your dog just wants to be alongside you, or is frightened of being left behind, but my experience tells me this is often not the case. She is frustrated at not being able to control the situation and keep her family together.

A good leader sees it as their job to keep the team together. Leaving her alone prevents her from maintaining this leadership at this time. The good leader should be you and you need to take the responsibility away from her, to prevent her from feeling stressed.

Q2. Does your dog wait at the bottom of the stairs for you, or even follow you up?   YES or NO

If your answer is No, well and good, but pretty much the same reasoning as Question 1, if you answered Yes, your dog is given control over where you are. You can't go up or down without her knowing about it.

Q3. Does your dog choose the hallway as her preferred resting place?   YES or NO

The answer should be No. If the answer is Yes, it's worth remembering the hallway is the central hub to the home. No one comes in or out without your dog knowing about it. If she occupies it, you cannot go anywhere in the home without her knowing – you can't go up or down stairs, she can see generally many rooms in the house and knows exactly where you are at all times. Lying in the hall way allows your dog to become very much in control of her whole environment. This is a definite no-no and I believe it is one of the biggest causes of separation anxiety. It can also lead to territorial behaviour developing, particularly when people are entering the home.

Q4. Does your dog leave you and go off to another location in the house at times, once you are in and settled?   YES or NO?

The answer should be No. In leaving you, this is her choice, you are giving her the freedom to choose, and this again puts control of the environment, back in her paws, so to speak. Whatever room you are in if you wish to have your dog with you for 'some of the time', that is fine, but at all times the door to the room should remain closed, so she has no option but to stay with you. This is your call, not hers. If she insists on wanting to leave, then put her back in her den, (not the room she chooses) and close the door/gate on her so she cannot return to you, or wander. Most dogs who have been allowed to do this will react and protest, i.e., frustration will occur as you dare to close the door on her. Completing this exercise will solve question 3 as well

Q5. Does your dog lie at the top of the stairs?
YES or NO

The answer should be No. If your answer is Yes, your dog has really chosen a top spot. The top of the stairs is the highest lookout point, where she can keep tabs on everything that is going on. She knows what room you are in and where you might move to next, and the stairs in many homes allow a dog the advantage of watching a main entrance and exit, usually the front door too. This allows her to police it at all times, whether it is you who might leave through it, or someone else who may enter.

This yet again allows her more control over her environment making her feel everything is secure under her own watch. Of course this all falls apart once you leave her alone so you are not doing her any favours in allowing this to develop or continue.

Q6. Does your dog lie across doorways?   YES or NO

Hoping the answer is No but again, if it's a Yes, you cannot leave the room without her knowing that you are going, and nobody can get in.

Never step over your dog, if she is in the way of a threshold or even in your path. Make sure she moves and even if you could go round her, don't. Insist that she gets up out of the way, this is the respectful thing for her to do, and helps her to understand you and your presence. It also prevents a potential accident from happening, should she decide to move, just as you are stepping over her.

Q7. Is your dog's sleeping place as you had intended, when she first joined your family?   YES or NO

If you answered 'No', this means from the very beginning your dog got to choose (in her mind) where she sleeps, this was the very first step in creating a learning problem for your dog. She learned that persistence pays off and she has a right to choose what she wants to do. Quite often most people when they bring a puppy home, set up puppy's bed in the kitchen and are determined that, that is where she will sleep but, because puppy is screaming and everyone wants to get some sleep, by the second or third night it is decided that bringing puppy to the bedroom with the intention of moving her back out later, is a better plan. However, it's easy to see what the outcome of this will be; quite often puppy remains in the bedroom and never makes it back to the kitchen. If you answered Yes, congratulations that is an achievement.

It would make much more sense when first bringing your puppy home, to have her den in your bedroom at night and allow her to settle and acclimatize to you and your family, without feeling alone. Once puppy has adjusted to this and is sleeping through the night without waking up, you can gradually move the den from your bedroom to your desired location (for more details see Chapter 13 Creating a Den).

Questions 8, 9 and 10 are probably the main contributing factors to separation anxiety.

Q8. Is your dog's movement restricted at night time?   YES or NO

If your answer is Yes, well done! If your answer is No, read questions 9 and 10 before reading the answer.

Q9. Is your dog's movement restricted when you are out of the home? YES or NO

If your answer is Yes, well done! If your answer is No, read question 10 before reading the answer.

Q10. Is your dog free to wander around when you are at home in the day time? YES or NO

If you answered Yes, then this is a big part of the problem. Free to wander and sleep where she chooses in the day time and then restricting her movements as in Questions 8 and 9 confuses the mind. It means your dog probably feels she should not be left alone if she can follow you throughout the day and keep tabs on where you are, why can't she do it at night, and you have no right to go out and leave her.

You are creating a dependency that she should have company at all times and that you must not leave the home ever without her.

Q11. Does your dog stay by you or even lie on you when she is with you? YES or NO

In answering Yes, dogs that need to make constant contact can become very needy, dependent and can be insecure. They can start to feel that they cannot function with you present and that they need to be touching you all the time, or have you touch them all the time. Sometimes this dependency can lead to possessiveness, another entire problem on its own.

The problem is, we humans seem to like this needy behaviour and love to be loved by our dogs needing to be with us. This can be our feel good factor. As a species, humans tend to nurture insecurity, but this is not helpful for dogs. This can cause a huge problem long term for you and your dog and can lead to developing many unwanted behaviours. No matter how much you love her, you are not helping her by encouraging this behaviour and you may just be creating a very insecure and therefore unhappy dog. Answering No could mean your dog has an air of confidence and independence.

If your dog has a crate/den or small sleeping area, then please answer these questions.

Set 2
Assess your dog's use of the crate/den.

Q1. Does she go into the den happily?

a) All the time?

b) Some of the time?

c) It is always a battle?

A Crate/Den should be a place of security and her safe haven. If your answer is a) Congratulations!

If you answered b or c, this means she isn't happy going into her den, some retraining is needed to make the den a more positive experience. Please refer to Chapters (12 and 13) 'Like it or Loathe it...' for full details of den training.

Q2. When does she use her den?

a) At bedtime?

b) When you go out?

c) Every time she sleeps?

(You may have answered any 1 or all 3)

Your answer should be c -- every time she sleeps, whether it is daytime, evening and bedtime.

Until she is happy, contented and relaxed, when left alone, the only place she should sleep is in her den. Den-time should be the norm, not the occasional, if you want a dog that is settled and not stressed at being left.

Q3. When you are preparing to leave your dog home alone, do you notice her starting to get anxious when you?

a) Pick up your keys?

b) Put your coat on?

c) Lock the windows?

Your answer could have been a, b, or c.

There may be many triggers that alert your dog that they are about to be left home alone. Each trigger must be dealt with individually to help disassociate them with an unpleasant experience.

For full details on teaching your dog to be home alone, go to Chapter 08 Helping your dog overcome their Separation Anxiety.

It is my hope that you have a better understanding of your dog and what is causing her to feel so anxious and stressed about being left alone.

08 Helping your dog to overcome their Separation Anxiety

In this chapter

- Round one – Learning to stay in a room without following you
- The Importance of keeping quiet
- Round two – Helping your dog to relax in their own company

Whether your dog's SA is caused through fear or frustration it is critical that you work through reshaping this behaviour using the following step by step procedure.

It is import not to miss out any steps if you are to achieve complete success for your dog.

Round One - Learning to stay in a room without following you

1. Start by accustoming your dog to having a door closed or baby gate closed when you leave the room. The best time to start this is just after she has been for a walk, so that she is tired and ready to settle for a sleep. The more

frequently you carry this out the better and the faster you will see results.

2. Ideally have your dog in the kitchen with you and practice going through to another room from the kitchen, so that she is left behind in the kitchen, as this is probably going to be the best place for her to remain when you are gone. Go in and out of the door/gate as many times as you can in an hour, always close the door behind you preventing the dog from following.

3. When you return through the door/ gate, do not speak to the dog or acknowledge that she is there. **No praising**, even if she is leaping all over you. To begin with she will try to follow you, act as though nothing is happening, but block her efforts, so that she can't get through the door. If you carry this out frequently enough your dog will tire of this and eventually give up trying to follow you. Not allowing your dog to follow you is the key to success here.

4. The point of this exercise is to tell your dog it is your decision to go where you want to go and that she doesn't get to be with you unless you invite her to be there.

5. Gradually increase the time you are out of the kitchen, make yourself a cup of tea and drink it in another room, take a visit to the bathroom, walk upstairs and back down again. Just move about and go back to her frequently to acclimatize her to not having access to follow you, at the same time building up her confidence. I cannot stress enough how important this exercise is.

6. If your dog starts to cry, say nothing. If she is very loud and you are concerned about the noise, make a noise to

distract her, as soon as she is quiet, even for a second, return to her, but don't praise her. Do not speak or make eye contact with her, just go back in and walk away again. Be aware that some dogs may become extremely fractious when this is happening, climbing, screaming and grabbing onto you when you return, as if you have been away for a week.

It is important that you 'keep calm and carry on'. Do not react to her, do not tell her off, as this will add to the anxiety and do not laugh, as this will excite her. If she is the fractious type, take very small steps with this stage, just in and out the gate repeatedly, until you see her start to accept this and calm down.

The importance of keeping quiet

You may be wondering why you aren't praising her at this stage; praise will reinforce her anxiety if it is timed incorrectly. Just because she is quiet, does not mean she is not anxious and it can draw attention to the fact that something different is happening. She will also read anxiety in your voice. Praise is not necessary to help her understand what she needs to do. This is often the hardest part for an owner to do, Keep Quiet.

She needs to learn that this is normal and there is nothing to worry about. Not talking makes you harder to read, and she will watch you closely and take her confidence from your body language. When she has settled and had her first sleep (and she will, but you must be more determined than her), it is important that you bring her out from the kitchen to join you before she asks to come out, even if it means waking her up.

Round Two – Helping your dog to relax in their own company

Reshaping SA, must begin by helping your dog to relax in her own company the following stages will take you through this process.

It is very important that you practice being able to put your dog in another room, while you go about your business elsewhere in the house. She doesn't need to see you and she does not need reassurance.

So, you have invited her into the lounge with you and you encourage her to settle with you or to play, whichever is appropriate for her energy levels. Ideally if you play with her for 20 mins to ½ an hour, it will be easier to settle her.

1. While your dog is with you in the living room, get up and call her to follow you to the kitchen. If she follows you, tell her she's a good girl and give her a treat. It is better if she follows you, rather than having to take her, so rattle her treats or do whatever it takes to get her to come to you. If she really does not want to follow you then lead her into the kitchen, if necessary use a slip lead and bring her through to avoid confrontation which can happen if you take hold of the collar and pull her.

2. Once in the kitchen, put a treat on her bed and while she is occupied eating, leave her there and go to another room, closing the door or the gate behind you.

You are going to do this exactly as in Round One. Straight in and out repeatedly at first until she stops reacting.

3. Don't leave her for any length of time at first so that the experience doesn't over stress her.

4. This will take a lot of repetitions, so please be patient. It is critical that you don't speak or acknowledge her, even if she is jumping on you for affection, do not give in and stroke her, as this will compound the problem.

5. If you cannot put your dog into another room of the house at your discretion, your dog is never going to be completely relaxed about being left whenever you need it to happen. This is a key stage to master to create a happy, confident, and well-adjusted home alone dog.

6. When you re-enter the room, do not allow her to jump on you to get close to you. **You must repeat this process, as many times in the day as you can**, this should be a normal occurrence and not an occasional occurrence, so that your dog becomes familiar with the new routine.

7. Once your dog accepts this new practice, and stops protesting when you leave the room, you will know she is starting to adjust to the new house rules.

As with Round One, when you reach this stage and you walk in the door to find her still sitting or lying where you left her, gently tell her she is a good dog, you may even offer her a treat, but always on her bed. Do not make a big fuss, just keep it calm, better to say less, than draw too much attention to the fact she was left.

8. Gradually increase the length of time you wait before you enter back into the room.

9. Under no circumstances must your dog be allowed to follow you around the home. You should be able to come and go as you please without your dog protesting, this is the only way to solve your dog's separation anxiety.

10. Every time your dog needs to sleep she must sleep in her own bed, away from you so she cannot follow you around in the daytime. **This is such an important step.** Once she learns to sleep separated from you in the daytime, and accepts where you put her, I guarantee you, she will no longer have a problem with you leaving her. I believe this to be the single cause of separation anxiety caused through 'frustration'.

11. You will help her and yourself enormously if you don't let her sleep in your bedroom at night. She needs continuity with her bed/den in the same room, i.e. kitchen/utility room at this stage.

12. If you live in a small apartment or flat and your dog's den is a crate and has to be in the same room as you then use a blanket to cover the crate, when she is in it at all times so that she cannot watch where you are going. This will help her to relax, at the same time blocking dependency from developing.

09 Help for Fear-based Separation Anxiety

In this chapter

- A different emotion calls for a different approach
- Door keys or car keys, what is your dogs' trigger?
- A place to call her own
- Working together

I am not huge fan of providing things for dogs to eat and chew on when left alone, as this can lead to its own set of problems i.e. the dog drinks more therefore needs to toilet more frequently, it also encourages them to be active rather than rest when left.

Also, if a dog is left unsupervised with a bone or a toy, there is the possibility of the dog choking on the bone (dogs have powerful jaws and bones can easily splinter) or toys etc. However, if a dog is to be left unsupervised, especially for a dog with extreme fear based separation anxiety, it is better in the early stages of behaviour modification, to have its attention directed to something else, but you will need to carry out a risk assessment in order to help the dog overcome its problem.

A different emotion calls for a different approach

Dealing with fear based separation anxiety, must be handled differently than the separation anxiety caused through frustration.

Helping your dog focus on something other than what is going on around her is important, sterile bones stuffed with something tasty is a good option, peanut butter (low salt), cream cheese etc. A Kong™ can be used for the same purpose (a Kong™ is a rubber toy that is designed for keeping dogs amused, it has a hollow centre which you can fill with food to encourage your dog to chew on it. They are supplied by '*The Company of Animals*', and are readily available online and in most pet shops. However, I find that dogs will chew on a natural bone longer than they will a rubber toy. Also, many dogs do not like rubber, my dogs will not attempt play with a rubber toy, let alone chew on one, so you may need to experiment a little.

It is important to remember that when a dog is very stressed they often refuse to eat, so it may be futile offering a bone in the early stages, but using the bone to overcome triggers can help redirect the early signs of stress. Together we are going to attempt to break down the fear triggers that alert panic in your dog.

Choose whichever trigger you have identified through the questions you answered earlier, as alerting your dog to your leaving.

Door keys or car keys? What is your dog's trigger?

1. *Go to your keys and touch your keys and move away from them again. Your dogs' attention may be alerted, don't look at her or speak to her, just carry on as though nothing happened.*

2. *Once she has settled down again, repeat the process. You need to keep doing this as many times as you can without going anywhere. However, you may find depending on how severe your dogs' anxiety is, that it takes her a long time, possibly an hour or so to settle because you touched*

the keys. You must be patient and if you only do this 2 or 3 times in a day that is fine.

3. *Once she has accepted you touching them and not going anywhere, try picking them up and moving them from one place to another.*

4. *Do exactly the same as before, move them then leave them in the new location. When she has settled, move them again. When she has stopped reacting, go to her, sit down beside her and offer calm praise as affection.*

5. *You are going to repeat the process but this time pick them up and put them in your pocket, then go sit down.*

6. *You are going to build this up until you can pick them up and walk out of the room and back in.*

You need to repeat this process with each trigger, whether it is brushing your hair, putting your coat on and taking it off again etc. Your commitment is the key to helping your dog overcome her fear of being left.

A place to call her own

As in the first section on separation anxiety it is now even more important that the fearful dog is provided with a small den area that becomes her secure haven. Also follow the steps on getting her used to you, moving about without following you. The difference here with fear as a base for this anxiety, is the use of the chew item. You are going to introduce this and build up the association that you leaving will mean goodies to chew on.

It is very important that the chew item is something that your dog really, really wants. You should have experimented with this before attempting to reshape this behaviour.

1. *Give her the stuffed bone/Kong™ and allow her to settle chewing on it. When she is really getting into chewing it, get up and move across your room towards the door.*

2. *If she gets up to follow you, calmly walk back to where the bone is, pick it up and put it away for a while and sit down.*

3. *Approximately an hour later, give her the bone again, let her settle and get up and go into another room, but make sure you return straight away. Every time you return to the room, you are going to take the bone away.*

4. *Taking the bone away upon your return will teach her that your return means end of pleasant experience and your departure means something good for her.*

Over time she should start to look forward to your leaving rather than dread it. How quickly your dog starts to change its patterns is determined by how consistent and frequently you act out the triggers. It could take a week, several weeks or a few months, depending on the severity of your dog's behaviour. Patience and commitment is going to be your greatest friend during this time.

Often people will say, 'We can't close him in the kitchen because he scratches the door and we don't want the door damaged'. While I appreciate you may not want the door damaged, this is not a good enough reason to not teach your dog to be comfortable being left. So I suggest if you don't want to use a crate, (which will of course avoid all damage to your home), you invest in a baby gate, so that this removes that problem, if you think your dog will jump a child gate, then buy the dog gate which is much taller.

Top Tip: If your dog gets stressed very quickly, it is important that you break everything down into smaller stages and succeed one step at a time, don't try to run before you can walk.

Working Together

As we have already explored at the beginning, SA can be an indication that your dog has been allowed to control her environment, by coming and going where and when she wants, throughout the home. It is crucial that you and your dog learn to work together so that you understand each other. Unfortunately your dog has no control over helping you to understand her; it is up to you to make the effort.

By the time people have contacted me for help with SA, their problems are often fairly desperate. The phone-call usually goes something like this,

'She is a wonderful dog, I have no problems with her except for this one,' whatever that may be.

For the record, it is never 'just' that problem, it may be the one problem that bothers you, and you don't want to live with it anymore, but it will often be symptomatic of something else that's going on in the relationship between you and your dog. You cannot treat the one problem in isolation. Any training program will fail if the whole picture is not looked at; it is often only a piece in the jigsaw.

It is for this reason, when people email me and say, 'What can I do about this problem?' Often the only answer I can give is, "I'm sorry but it will need a Behavioural Consultation to solve this." The problem they've described to me is often only a small part of the bigger picture.

10 How to Prevent your Rescue Dog from developing Separation Anxiety

In this chapter

- Introducing a rescue dog into your home
- Providing a security blanket – fit for a dog
- Give them what they need, not what you think they need
- The time of arrival – what to remember

Taking on a rescue dog into your home is such a rewarding experience but it sometimes comes with its own set of problems. Dogs end up in rescue for all manner of reasons, marital break ups, and owner is deceased or moving home and can't take the dog and abandonment. Sometimes a dog has just not been given the correct training and they develop unwanted behaviour problems that the owner can no longer cope with. The dog is then handed over to a rescue centre but often the history isn't handed over with the dog. Which means the dog, if he or she is fortunate enough to be placed in a new home, is rehomed with little or no information and the problem usually unfolds at around the 4 months mark of settling into the new home.

Whatever the reason the dog is in the home, unless it is aggression it is often irrelevant as to how the dog will behave in your home. I have seen dogs with perfectly sweet temperaments and seemingly few issues come from rescue and within a 2 to 3 week period develop separation anxiety. This is caused by how the dog is introduced into the home and the environment the new owner has created for this dog.

Introducing a rescue dog into your home

When bringing a dog into your home which has fallen on hard times, we humans have a tendency to let emotions cloud what we should be doing, we usually over-compensate for the life they have had or the life we think they have had before.

The first thing that happens is, we give them the keys to the castle, and this grants them as much space as they want, because they have been 'cooped' up in a kennel. Then we lavish them with lots of luxuries.

While I know your intentions are good and you want to love that dog and make it very happy, neither of these things are in the best interest of the dog and space to roam around is usually the last thing they need right at that moment.

They need security, they need a small area where they can feel that they belong and take time to adjust to this new life, filled with new people, sights and smells. Many dogs struggle to cope with space and can go into serious panic mode, which leads to weeing, pooing, chewing and barking, some are completely freaked out by all this space and experience a feeling of abandonment all over again.

My advice to people taking on a rescue dog is always the same, you don't need to know her past to live with or understand her. As mentioned earlier, dogs are adaptable. She will mould to her new environment and to your family if you show her where she fits in.

Providing a security blanket - fit for a dog

Restricting her freedom is the best gift you can give to her right now. A bit like being wrapped in a blanket, she will feel secure.

People are always eager to know what has happened to the dog and often try to look for clues in the dog's body language, for what it has gone through, but this is often wrongly interpreted. When faced with a rescue dog in a consultation, the most common line I hear is, 'We think she has been beaten'. I ask what evidence there is to back this up. I will get various responses. She doesn't like men, she growls at them or hides. She runs away if you pick up a brush or attacks it. Now she may well have been beaten, but it is just as probable that the dog is unfamiliar with these things and is therefore wary of them or overreacts to them. She may have not been taught it is wrong to attack the brush in her first home, she may have been raised by a woman and had little contact with men. Whatever her reasons for her reactions, they are irrelevant to how she lives now.

Forget them, let go, stop trying to unravel her past and allow her to move forward. She will move on if you move on, when she sees these things are not a problem for you, she will gain confidence and start to trust you to lead her.

Give them what they need, not what you think they need

The best home you can give a rescue dog is the home 'they' need. Security of knowing where they belong and that there are rules, boundaries and a set structure to follow, they are after all a creature of habit. Give them these things and you will create a happy contented dog that thrives on their bond with you, and looks to you for direction.

If you are just embarking upon getting a rescue dog there are a couple of simple guidelines you should follow to prevent problems from arising. However I am fairly certain that most people will ignore these guidelines as it is not how they want to live with their new dog, but this is a temporary measure to allow your new dog to become comfortable with who you are, where she lives and now belongs and where she fits in. These things matter to her, set yourself aside and allow her to find her place, it is the best gift you can give her.

The time of arrival, remember –

1. From the day your dog comes into your home, give her a secure area and keep her to it for at least a week or two before you allow her to explore another room in the house.

2. Only when she is happy to stay in this location do you allow her to come into another room with you, but she doesn't get to sleep in it nor occupy it when you are not there.

3. Depending on the dog, you may need to stay in the first room with her to begin with, until she adjusts and settles, before you start leaving her for short periods. Make her

den a pleasant experience, by rewarding her with treats and things to chew on and also feed her dinner in it.

4. Do not bring her into your home and allow her to wander around and explore everywhere. Without you realising it she could be freaking out inside, because she is unsure of the new surroundings, she doesn't know the smells of you or this new place yet.

5. She needs time to adjust to your smell and one room before going anywhere near the other room/s. She is a dog with a keen sense of smell, she can smell from a distance what else awaits her.

6. She must only be allowed to fall asleep in the secure area, nowhere else, not even at your feet, as this can create dependency, leading to further problems like separation anxiety.

If you already have a rescue dog that has developed Separation Anxiety, you need to follow the steps as outlined starting in Chapter 10 – *Helping your dog to overcome SA*.

11 How to Prevent your New Puppy from developing Separation Anxiety

In this chapter

- What your puppy needs
- Sleep time
- Why her own space is so important

Whether you are planning on a puppy coming into your world, or already have your puppy, prevention is always better than cure. A very true saying when working with dogs and my answer to preventing it is, Restriction, Restriction, Restriction. I cannot stress this enough with new puppy owners and I will probably keep stressing it.

Puppies have a natural in built, follow the leader mechanism between 6 to 13 weeks old. As puppy grows and matures this will become less as she learns how to take charge of situations herself, you must harness this instinct in order to raise a balanced dog that looks to you for guidance.

We all have the ideal picture in our heads, of our family dog, roaming free through the house, living peacefully alongside the family. This ideal picture can come with time, but is not recommended in the early stages of training a puppy.

What your puppy needs

Your puppy needs a space that is her home, a crate, a pen, or even a small room. This is going to be where your puppy/young dog lives until all the house rules have been established. This will be your puppy's den until she reaches maturity, which may take as long as 18 months to 2 years. Some breeds take longer than others to mature and it may even mean restrictions until they are 3 or 4 years old. Patience is essential if you are to avoid unwanted problems developing.

Sleep Time

Your puppy should only be allowed to sleep in her area and nowhere else in the house. This provides continuity and leaves your dog in no doubt as to, who the house belongs to, as well as where she fits in.

By teaching your dog to enjoy her own space and relax in her own company and routinely go to sleep in it, you create the habit for her and dogs are naturally a creature of habit.

Why her own space is so important

Your puppy has her area where she is allowed to play, eat and sleep. - Sleep is the key word here. This is where people make the biggest mistake.

A Scenario: Puppy is running around playing, then puppy gets tired and she wanders off to find a spot to sleep. This becomes the normal pattern very quickly. Wherever your puppy sleeps, becomes hers (in her mind). It becomes her right to choose where she sleeps, in a relatively short space of time, you will find she starts to object to being asked to go into her crate or den, because you have allowed her to believe it is for her to choose. As I said, dogs are a creature of habit, if the only place they are allowed to sleep is their crate, they will never object to it, they will love it and look forward to switch off time.

Every time she needs to sleep, show her to her crate. This is a huge advantage while raising a puppy, it gives you a better start on toilet training, as puppy can't wake up and wander off for a wee without your knowing about it. This will teach her to ask you to let her out.

If your puppy has joined your home and you already have a resident dog, it is even more important to follow a set structure. Your pup must sleep where you put her and not be allowed to sleep with the other dog, no matter how cute it may seem and no matter how accepting your other dog may be of the puppy.

Your puppy should not get a choice, otherwise you may have a puppy that not only can't be without your company, but also walks in the shadow of your other dog and cannot function well as an individual.

Many people appear to like it when their dogs' become inseparable from each other, for me I find it rather sad. One or other of the dogs can become very unbalanced and almost appear neurotic when this happens, it creates so many problems that it would need another book to unfold them.

I meet so many people who will say to me, *"They are inseparable"*, or *"Where one goes the other is right behind"*, or the favourite, *"He protects her, he doesn't let anyone near her"*.

In my opinion, none of these are good scenarios. The minute you have a dog who behaves like this you are not in control of the situation, no matter how much you think you are. Things are likely to go wrong very quickly and your dogs are looking to each other, and not to you for guidance, which at some point is very likely to lead to problems, that could have been avoided. They may be problems that don't bother you and you are happy to live with them, but that is another matter and does not necessarily mean because you are ok with them, that your dogs are happy.

If you are not in favour of crate training, you should still come up with a location within your home, the kitchen, utility room, down stairs loo, or a puppy pen, where your puppy can be restricted. She must be separated from your other dog and not have freedom to follow it or you around. Remember, this is not going to last forever, the restriction is there to provide you with the dog you want long term; a confident, balanced and relaxed family pet.

For full details of den training read the next chapter Like it or Loathe it...

12 Like it , or Loathe it – at least try to understand Den Training

In this chapter

- Providing your dog with a secure area to relax
- What is a suitable small location for your puppy?
- Why den training works
- A successful SA story – Chaotic Ciro
- My recommendations for Ciro

Providing your dog with a secure area to relax

For me one of the best concepts in dog training was the creation of Den/Crate training. This provided our dogs with a secure resting place, somewhere they rest undisturbed; when they are in their den or crate they are secure in the knowledge they are doing the right thing.

For us, the den/crate keeps our furry friend out of trouble when we aren't there to supervise which in turn keeps them safe.

Whether you like it or loathe it, crate training is a huge part of dog training. I am well aware that there are those who believe crate training is cruel, unnatural and unnecessary and that is their choice. For me this is not a rational way of thinking, dogs are domesticated and as I have already said, they are adaptable. They accept what they know and are often wary of the unfamiliar.

If we want to talk about what is natural for a moment, then digging a hole in the ground as a den to sleep in is quite natural, this enables three sides of the dog to be protected, or crawling under a hide out, but this is not practical for our delightful house dogs, so we are offering her a chance to have a little of the security that is 'natural', by offering her a homemade den.

What is a suitable small location for your puppy?

As mentioned earlier, if you are not in favour of using a crate for den training, you must still come up with a location within your home, the kitchen, utility room, down stairs loo etc., where your dog can be restricted.

Notice my suggested locations are mostly places found to the rear of many properties. Ideally your dogs' den should be located away from your entrance and exit. Not being able to see you leave the house will lower any anxiety they may have. The same applies to looking out through windows. It is seldom if ever, a good idea to allow dogs; the same view that you or I would enjoy, i.e. to look out a window. All too often, the causes territorial behaviour to raise its head, it also adds to her anxiety if she can see people coming and going or passing the house. This almost always creates a dog who barks; your dog believes she is protecting the house as people appear to move away while she is barking. It's the equivalent to her thinking she has seen them off.

My suggested locations are also small. Small is always best for your dog. The less room she has to wander around, the less pacing she will do and the less likely she is to need to toilet or become anxious. Wandering around is a guaranteed way to stimulate bladder and bowel movements.

Remember, this is not going to last forever, this restriction on your dog, is to help your dog fit with your family and provide you with the dog you want long term. You are shaping your dog into a confident, contented companion for you and your family.

Why den training works

I always prefer to refer to this as 'den training', to help those of you who are uncertain about the concept of crating your pup/dog. Any dog can learn to adjust to a den, even an adult, I have helped many dogs who have had various issues from separation anxiety to toilet issues or destruction issues over many years. All have learned to accept and love their den. Even older dogs, take Ciro as an example.

A successful SA story - Chaotic Ciro

Ciro was a very large black German Shepherd with extreme Separation Anxiety. When Belinda, (Ciro's owner) contacted me, her telephone conversation was pretty desperate. In fact her words to me were, "You are my last hope, and if you can't help he will have to go".

When I first met Ciro I was shocked at the devastation that lay in his wake, there was no wall paper on the walls as high as he could reach, the kitchen cupboard doors were hanging of the hinges, the couch was just a shell, the internals of which were all over floor, including the arm of the couch, which Belinda promptly picked up and put back inside the couch while offering me the seat. I then realised there was no living room door, it was standing propped up against the wall, Belinda caught my eyes glance at the door and without prompting said "Yes, that's his handy work too, I went out and came back to it lying on the floor and he'd even stripped half the door frame with it'.

I have to admit, I was so tempted to laugh; it seemed unbelievable that one dog could cause the devastation I was seeing, somehow I didn't think Belinda would share my humour, so I resisted the urge. Oh and not forgetting the tall fridge that no longer worked; Belinda explained how she returned home from shopping to find him sitting inside the fridge with the rubber seal in his mouth, the entire contents had gone.

This was a very small flat that they shared. Belinda told me she had bought new furniture which was stored in an adjacent room but couldn't bring it in until she knew he wouldn't destroy it, which right at that moment was a very real possibility.

Approximately 3ft from where I stood were patio doors, leading to a small, walled yard and there stood Ciro, pressed up against the glass making sure he could see who had entered his world. He looked excited, panting furiously, frustrated and curious. I couldn't wait to meet him. Just as I was about to ask Belinda to let him in, she said, "He'll kick off in a minute".

I enquired as to what she meant by that, Belinda replied, "He does anything he can to get my attention, so that I open the door to tell him off and then he bursts in". No sooner had she said this when a plant pot was hurled at the doors, in the blink of an eye Ciro then made his move on the hose pipe, with the hose in his mouth he proceeded to unroll it from its reel at a very impressive speed.

Belinda banged on the glass doors to distract Ciro, at which point he promptly threw himself at the doors in disapproval of her objection, it was like thunder going off with the effort he put in.

'I think it's time to meet him' I said. Belinda hesitantly replied 'Are you sure? He's nuts and he will bounce you'.

Well I have to say that, that was an understatement, I placed myself firmly on the edge of the couch, sitting back was not an option, for fear of falling through and I braced myself as the doors slid back. He entered the room like a whirlwind and greeted me as a long lost relative. It was at this point that I *gave in and chuckled, although keeping composure as all good dog trainers/behaviourists should.*

At this particular time the German Shepherd Dog as a breed, didn't have a particularly good reputation, there had been more than a few incidents of attacks by the breed, this boy was so friendly, and Ciro was certainly a good advert for the breed. He didn't have one ounce of suspicion in him. He was a 2½ year old, full of pent up energy, excitement and fun that had no outlet for what he was feeling.

As a Canine Behaviourist, I have always been very hands on in my approach to dealing with problems. I like to see the dog behave as naturally as possible so that I can have first-hand knowledge and experience of the intensity of the dog and its problem. Often the problem as described by the owner is something entirely different when the dog shows it to me.

Ciro was on me, over me, behind me, and there was just no calming, no matter how much you ignored this dog he was not calming down. He was hyper with a capital H. He had zero manners and was quite a liability with his level of exuberance. He had no idea of rules and boundaries neither with the home or those around him, even the cats where fair game for which he bore many a scar.

I calmly took hold of his collar and removed him from behind me from the couch to the floor to which, surprisingly, he made no objection, and he sat down in front of me and looked at me, weighing up this new person who had asked him for something different. He was receptive to being handled and taking instruction. Ciro could not contain his enthusiasm; there was just no outlet for this beautiful working dog to use his mental and physical energy.

Ciro's separation anxiety had grown out of pure frustration. As a puppy Ciro spent all his time with Belinda, travelling to work with her, but very quickly he outgrew the workplace and he had to be left at home. Belinda was unaware that because Ciro had been given so much companionship and control, he did not feel it was her place to leave him alone.

He was her guardian and leader and was frustrated at not being allowed to do his job. Belinda also revealed that when she takes him in the car he was good at being left in it, but this could not happen in the summertime, because of the heat, so she had no option but to leave him home alone and this is when it all started to go wrong.

My recommendations for Ciro

I suggested an increase in training and exercise, and that we should introduce a den/crate for Ciro as he needed somewhere that he could learn to switch off, but before Ciro could be expected to rest in a crate, he must receive whatever exercise he needed to tire him, he was a very active, very frustrated young dog.

I was conscious of the size of the flat and that we were going to need a fairly large crate to house Ciro, however Belinda's response was what every Behaviourist wants to hear; "I will do whatever it takes". That very same day at Belinda's request, a large crate was installed and yes it did take up a lot of space in the small lounge, but from the minute I put it up Ciro went in and lay down, it was what he had been longing for, a place he could go and switch off; somewhere he knew he belonged.

With an increase in exercise and training, Ciro stopped all the destruction within one week. I received a very tearful phone call from Belinda telling me how grateful she was that Ciro was now so happy and the redecorating had begun on the flat. All I could say to Belinda was 'Thank you for not giving up on him and giving him what he needed'. I am always amazed at how much some people will tolerate in their dog's behaviour but then there are others who give up so easily.

13 Creating a Den

In this chapter

While not all cases are this simple to solve as Ciro's, many are. It is important to know what your dog needs and to fulfil those needs. Fortunately more and more people are realising the sense in den training, which leads to quicker toilet training and prevents undesirable behaviours from developing such as in Ciro's story.

To date I have not known a dog who was introduced to the den 'correctly' who didn't love their new secure bed.

The den should be just big enough for your dog to stand up, turn round and lie down. Too big a crate may encourage your dog to toilet at one end of it and this is a highly undesirable trait to encourage.

A den is a place that allows your dog freedom to rest undisturbed when she chooses and when you need her to. It also allows you the peace of mind in knowing your dog is not getting up to mischief when you can't watch her, a bit like putting a baby into a play pen or cot. It's for their-own safety.

What does a den look like?

The den can be a wire crate, a *Vari Sky Kennel (TM)*, a cupboard with the door removed, it may even be a small room. There are various options. It's a secure area for your dog.

Quite often, dogs or puppies will choose to make their bed under a table or behind the settee, the den you choose offers a better alternative than this. The den you provide is your chosen area for your dog rather than your dog choosing the area. This is more likely to prevent territorial issues from developing.

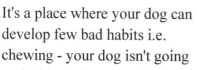

It's a place where your dog can develop few bad habits i.e. chewing - your dog isn't going to decide to chew your table leg or climb on the work surfaces when you're not around if he's in a den.

Your dog will learn to switch off and sleep when you're out shopping or at work, making him a more contented friend.

The den will be your dog's bed. Dogs do not like to soil their beds which means they will cry when they need to go out.

If you have a dog who has previously had a bad experience with crate training, and you would rather not revisit crate training then please look for an alternative location, as suggested to you previously.

Introducing the den

The den to some people is a new concept and for others it has been in use for years. In training there are various ideas and ways to teach your dog to accept and enjoy her own den.

If you haven't had experience of the concept of den training and how it works, you may take a little convincing that you want to use it for your dog keep an open mind.

I recommend den training to most owners. They are suitable for both puppies and for the older dog too. The first reaction I get from people is sometimes one of shock; some are even horrified at the thought of putting their dog into what seems like a 'cage'. It may take a little time, but once people have stopped thinking of the crate as a cage and more as a den, most agree to try it out.

Without exception I have never had anyone regret using the den. Most usually say they can't imagine living without one. The mistake some people make, is taking the den away from the dog too soon in her development i.e. before puppy has fully matured, which sometimes means she relapses into unwanted behaviours such as chewing and toileting indoors. So please don't dismiss this very successful system of training which provides your dog with security and contentment, knowing that she has her own safe haven. At least not until you understand all the benefits of what is 'den training.'

The following method of den training has proven completely successful for me in my years as a dog trainer.

To help your dog accept and love their den, please remember these important points:

- The den must always be associated with something good.
- Give the introductions slowly.
- The den must never be used for punishment.
- The den must never be used because you haven't got time to play, train or work with your dog.

Stage 1 - How to make a den exciting for your dog

1. Have the den in the same room as the family, i.e. Living area or wherever most of the family are present.

2. Put a comfortable blanket or large towel in the den.

3. Secure the door of the den open, so that it doesn't move which could scare your puppy or dog. Many dogs learn to dislike the crate because of a bad introduction like being caught by the door, prevention is always better than cure.

4. Play with your dog by the den. If at first your dog appears scared of the den when he approaches it, begin by playing with a favourite toy near to the den. Start by throwing the toy near to the den/crate and allow her to fetch it and work up to throwing her toy or a treat into it, allowing her to enter and fetch it. Don't force her to go in if she is hesitant.

5. A chew that your dog likes to gnaw on is also a good idea, often they want to lie in a secure area to eat it. The den is the ideal place for this.

6. Have some small morsels of food and throw them into the den encouraging your dog to go in and out of the den, until she is completely happy with entering the den. You may have to use meat as a definite appetiser, rather than a dog treat, to encourage her to go in. Depending upon your dog's character will determine how long it takes to get over this.

Stage 2 - Feeding in the den

1. Introduce your dog's meal times in the den, but only if she has accomplished stage 1 and is happy going into it.

2. As she enters the den introduce a command like 'den', 'bed' or 'place'.

3. When she starts to eat, gently close the door and let her finish eating. Once finished open the door and let her out. Do not move away or leave her while she is eating at this stage.

4. If, when you put the meal in the den and the dog refuses to enter, bring the meal nearer to the entrance and allow your dog to get used to the idea and eat with just her head in the crate if she is wary. Keep your hand on the bowl, to give her confidence.

5. I don't find puppies have a problem with eating in the den, as they generally have no suspicion of it. It is usually more of a problem with the adult dog who has some experience of being closed in or, she has a fear of the unfamiliar.

6. If you are able to close the door while she eats, open it straight away and allow her to come out and take her to the toilet if she needs to go when she is finished.

Stage 3 – Getting your dog accustomed to sleeping in the den

This is the single most important step for teaching your dog what you want from her.

It is crucial that your dog is tired before working on this next stage. So make sure she has been for a long walk/run or played for sufficiently to tire her.

1. When you see her settle down to sleep on the floor, encourage her to go in the den and stay with her until she settles.

2. It is crucial that there is no other dog bedding around the home, so that there is only one option for sleeping comfortably, the den.

3. Do not close the door of the den until she has settled to sleep. You can offer affection while she is sitting or lying in the den, but if she seems to be settling then leave her peacefully to get on with it.

4. If she comes out of the den, do not share affection with her at this time, and don't try to stop her from coming out, or you will panic her.

5. If she comes out and lies down on the floor, encourage her to come back to the den, you can pick her up and put her into it, if she is small enough, if she is on the large size, use a treat to entice her in.

Please note, you should only feed treats in the den (and never out of it) *at this stage in training*.

Achieving the first sleep in the den is the hardest step, but be more determined than she is and don't give up.

Pause for Thought:

At all times when the dog is tired she must be encouraged to sleep in her den. Do not at this stage in training allow her to fall asleep on the floor or elsewhere. This is extremely important for the long term success of crate training. This communicates to your dog that it is your decision where she should sleep.

It is inevitable that at some point she is going to object to being in the den. Ignore her protest; do not tell her off. The minute she is quiet, even if it's only for a second, go to her and gently praise her. At this stage, you may wish to let her out and try again later.

Obviously with a puppy it is easier to get through this stage, as she will tire much quicker than an adult dog and she will care less about where she sleeps, than an adult dog, make sure she is sufficiently tired when you first introduce the den.

If she isn't settling in the crate and is protesting, she is probably not tired enough. Do something with her to tire her out, but don't let her sleep on the floor or anywhere else and then try again. If she is reluctant to get in the crate, here is a little exercise that will help kick start her into having positive feelings toward the crate and seeing it as a good thing.

1. Get a handful of small treats, try throwing some treats in, a couple at a time, and make sure she sees them go in. Then wait, she will go in, eat them, and walk out again.

2. When she has had a few goes, hold back on throwing treats in and watch her work it through, at some point she will eventually go to explore the crate-den, to see if there's anything in there.

3. Make a huge fuss of her and throw some treats in. keep repeating the process until she is going in on her own and looking round at you.

4. Eventually she will go in and she will sit down or lie down. Jack pot her with a handful of treats as soon as this happens. Hopefully this will be enough to plant in her mind that the crate is a positive thing.

The den should NOT be used as a place to put your dog so you don't have to bother with her. Some people choose to use the den for the whole of the dog's life, rather than wean them of it as their bed, this is absolutely fine, as long as you do not substitute the den for training or for allowing her to be part of the family. Most dogs prefer their own den (once they have accepted it) over any other bed.

If you decide you do not want her in the den forever then gradually introduce her to your preferred location i.e. kitchen, beginning when you are at home with her.

Taking the den away, is not recommend, until your pup has come through the puppyhood/adolescent stage, or at least an age where she can be trusted not to chew things, this is usually after two years, preferably three years.

Whatever location, you move your dog to in the home, there should still remain restrictions. The biggest mistake people make is to give the dog the free run of the house at this young age. This is a recipe for disaster.

As I have said before, dogs prefer the security of smaller spaces over being allowed to wander, despite what you might think. If you want to allow freedom in the home, you must do it gradually over months, even a year or two, only once you know your dog is relaxed, confident and trustworthy should freedom be given.

14 You return home to find a mess, what should you do?

In this chapter
- Successful SA story – Lonely Lola
- Sometimes an owner needs convincing
- The result from 3 simple steps

So what do you do, when you return home to find that your dog has toileted on your best rug, or destroyed something in the home that you can't replace? What should happen is, your dog should never be met with correction. To correct a dog that has made a mess in the home when left alone, is a sure fire way of creating anxiety for your dog when you leave home the next time.

I would be very rich if I had a pound for every time someone said, 'She knows what she has done, when I return she hides and will not come to me, because she has made a mess.'

I know this is difficult for you to accept, but our dogs don't know that the mess that came out of them is wrong. When a dog has to go, it has to go, particularly if stress is a trigger.

They don't know that chewing wood is wrong, it is what they do, and they explore things with their teeth when they are bored, when they are teething or to understand what it is. They don't know that digging the carpet is wrong, digging is what you do to hide or lie low, and it's what they do when you need to get to the other side of something.

What they do know is when there is something on the floor, wee, poo, wood paper etc. that your personality changes and they see something they don't understand and that is unpredictable to them, i.e. you get angry, so the best thing for them to do is avoid you when you come home. This is the hard truth of the matter, what they don't know is, it's because they made the mess that you are angry.

You need to change how you think if this is familiar to you. Often separation anxiety escalates from doing what comes naturally as a puppy, i.e. weeing and pooing, because you have reacted to it every time you see it. Let me tell you about Lola.

A Successful SA Story - Lonely Lola

Lola was a young Chocolate Labrador, about 10 months old. Lola and her owner Carol joined my dog training classes when Lola was approx. 13 weeks old.

For months they trained with me, and every week at question and answer time they had nothing to ask, everything seemed to be going fine. Then one week out of the blue, Carol said she had a problem.

Carol ran a clothing catalogue and Lola had torn up two of the deliveries that had been delivered by mail while she was out. This was starting to escalate and was now costing Carol a lot of money, as she had to pay for the damages and had a lot of unhappy customers.

Carol explained to me that, 'she knows it is wrong because she hides upstairs and won't come down when I come home'. Carol also explained that Lola had started pooing every time she was left and again she reiterated, 'she knows it is wrong'.

I asked Carol to explain to me what exactly she does, when she arrives home to find the mess. She said, I bring her to what she has done and show her it and then tell her off and I tell her how bad she is. I clean up the mess and don't speak to her for a while. She said Lola just lies with her head down and doesn't come near me as she knows I am really cross with her.

My recommendations for Lola in 3 simple steps

Sometimes an owner needs convincing and Convincing Carol that Lola did not understand what she had done, was really difficult, she was convinced otherwise and confident in what she thought she was seeing. So I asked her to help me with a little experiment. I asked her to follow these steps for me.

1. I asked her to ignore any mess that she should find on the floor, the next day she returned home. My instructions were to walk straight past the mess as though it wasn't there, don't even glimpse at it and speak to Lola to in a nice happy tone.

2. If Lola followed her to put her outside to the toilet then Carol should clear up the mess and bring Lola in and make a huge fuss of her, as though nothing had happened at all.

3. Repeat every day for a week.

Summary – 3 days that led to Lola's anxiety?

After just two days carrying out these steps, Carol returned home to find there was no mess and Lola was waiting to greet her with a waggy tail. She reported back to me in absolute amazement that Lola had stopped making a mess. So what happened to make Lola start toileting indoors?

Day One - A parcel came through the door, were Lola could investigate it, strange smells entered her territory, and her natural instinct led her to explore it further, opening the parcel and shredding the object. Nothing more than being inquisitive, the owner returns to see the mess and gives Lola a telling off.

Day Two - The next day is a repeat of the same. Owner returns and Lola receives another telling off.

Day Three - Lola starts to stress when she is about to be left, because of the previous experiences she has met with, when owner Carol returned. This stress causes Lola to need the toilet, which Lola receives another telling off for. And so the cycle begins.

Lola's stress had started to show before Carol had even left the house, this was because Lola now associates her owner leaving with her being told off on her return. The chances of Lola having a toilet accident, while being left home alone, are probably about 95% because her stress level is now so high. Take the stress level down and the accidents will stop happening. As for the tearing the post up, now that's another matter! And an easy solution would be to, a) put Lola where she can't access the front door, which would be my preferred option, or b) buy a post catcher on the back of the door.

As it happens Carol decided to relocate Lola towards the back of the house, where she could no longer watch the front door or become stressed by anything being delivered through the letter box. A win, win situation both for Lola and Carol. Carol could not believe the transformation in Lola, in such a short period of time.

This success story, is of course only one type of anxiety reaction, related to being left, and I am sharing it with you in the hope that you can see, how something so simple can trigger stress related behaviours in your dog and perhaps help you to think about your reactions when you discover your dog has done something you would rather she hadn't.

15 Can you go to work and own a dog?

In this chapter

- Dog walkers
- Doggy day-care or sitters

We all lead busy lives, many people who own dogs need to work. In fact few of us are in the fortunate position where we can just sit home and play with the dog. This may not be ideal for a dog, but it is reality and telling people they shouldn't have a dog because they work, isn't realistic. So in my mind the best option is to help people and more importantly help dogs to adjust to life with some time spent alone. Remember your job is to meet your dog's needs and it is essential that you get this right so that you don't have a frustrated or anxious dog.

If you work and own a dog, you need to remember, dogs are social animals and while it is ok to leave them for short periods, dogs do not cope well with being left alone for a 7 or 8 hours a day while you work. Even if you do leave your dog for this length of time and she doesn't seem to complain, this is not good practice on a daily basis, NO DOG should be left home alone for these amount of hours and if you feel you have no option then as you can't provide an alternative than perhaps you should re-think whether you should inflict your life on a dog.

Dog walkers

My recommendation is that your dog should not be left for more than 3 to 4 hours without company and a break from the environment. Even still, this only applies to an adult dog that has been raised and trained to deal with this. A puppy should never be left for more than 2 hours at a time. If you need to work for more than this length of time, I suggest you hire a dog walker to come in and take her out for at least an hour of good walking after 3 to 4 hours alone, to break up the day. Also, think about someone you could call who could tend to your dog in the event of an emergency, always have their number to hand in case you are delayed at work.

An important point to remember:

Make sure your dog walker is experienced, not just in walking dogs, but in dog behaviour, first aid and holds insurance.

Doggy day-care or sitters?

There is also the option of doggy day care. Your dog gets to meet with other dogs and has some company. There are many who do this in their homes now, however make sure they have the experience and expertise needed to deal with events that may arise, i.e., if they house multiple dogs what the procedure is should a fight break out. If you choose this option it is important you make sure the day care staff are, suitably qualified in understanding dogs and they carry out a play and rest regime.

It does not help your dog if he has company all day and never learns to rest on his own. This can cause you problems should you ever need to stop this service. Make sure the company is equipped to offer this, to avoid problems in the future and also make sure they are qualified to deal with multiple dogs.

What is their procedure if two dogs don't get on? Are they insured for your dog on and off the premises? What is their procedure in case of an accident? Ask questions; don't assume because they have a fancy name or a well-equipped van, that they know what they are doing.

You are responsible for making sure you leave your dog in safe hands. Also make sure that they are actually at home looking after your dog and not off out doing another job (it happens), they are being paid to care for your dog, providing for her physical and mental wellbeing.

Whoever you choose to care for your dog, make sure if they are going to take your dog for a run, where if she is going to

get wet, that they have the means to dry her before leaving her. It is very bad for your dog and her coat to be left to lie in a bed if they are soaking wet. They are likely to get early arthritis, not to mention, a very matted coat if left to dry like this.

16 Will getting a second dog make things better for your dog?

This is the 50 million dollar question. For some yes it may help, for others, definitely not.

There will always be someone who will tell you, "Get another dog, they are good company for one another".

This may work and it may not work, and you need to know that this is going to work before jumping in. If it doesn't work you will have big trouble on your hands, the chances are you will have double the noise + double the mess = twice the work in cleaning it up. Borrow a dog and test this theory before you go out and purchase a second dog and whatever you do, getting a puppy is probably not the best solution as a puppy is likely to do exactly what your adult dog is already doing, a puppy in all likelihood will add to your dogs' stress, not alleviate it.

Think very carefully before you opt for this option, some dogs may even be happy with the company of a cat, but again check this out, because it is not always guaranteed.

It is also important that you have at least decided, hopefully with the help of this book, what is triggering your dogs' anxiety, is she anxious about being alone? Or is she anxious that 'You' are not with her. If your dogs' Separation Anxiety is person specific, there is no point in bringing in another dog or cat, as this will definitely not solve your dog's problem and in all probability it will add to your problems.

17 Summary

Bringing a dog into our lives is not something that should be taken lightly. They have needs that must be met and learning how to cope and where they fit in, in our world is essential.

It is my hope that you have a better understanding of your dogs' problem, now that you have read this book. Separation Anxiety is a real problem for many of todays' dogs, but it doesn't have to be. They aren't born with it and it can be avoided. It is something that often is caused by us, with a few exceptions to the rule.

I hope that the methods in this book help you to help your dog become balanced and relaxed. We all want our dogs to want us, but it is not good for them to not be able to function without us, or without another dog by their side. The message that runs as a thread throughout this book, to help your dog and keep your dog balanced is restriction, restriction, restriction. Too much freedom, too soon, with no guidelines and boundaries proves to be a problem for many, many dogs, irrespective of their breed. Whether you have a Tibetan Terrier, a German Shepherd, or a Border Collie, Separation Anxiety is not part of their DNA. It is not genetic. Please don't blame it on the breed. Look at your life and your dog, look at what your dogs' needs and then ask yourself, what can I do to help my dog?

Be patient with the dog who is suffering from Separation Anxiety, but be firm and consistent, sympathy and emotion will not help a dog with this disorder. Dogs change when we change, they don't hang onto the past, that's a human concept and because we keep holding on we prohibit them from moving forward.

If you have a new puppy, you have no excuse; you are now armed with the tools to prevent this ever from happening. Remember if separation anxiety is to be avoided, what happens when you 'are at home' and not when you are out is the key. It is no good restricting your pup's movements when you are out and then letting her have constant free time when you are home, remember, this is the very thing that can trigger separation anxiety later on. It has a funny way of creeping up on you.

It is my hope that this book will reach all those with a dog or thinking about owning a dog. Even if your dog doesn't have separation anxiety and you own a dog, you should be aware of the journey that leads your dog to this disorder. Remember forewarned is forearmed.

It is Okay for your dog to be home alone, but not for an 8 hour day, your dog is a social animal, provide for her the companionship she needs, don't expect her just to fit your busy world or she will pay the price for that in stress and you will pay the price in more ways than one.

You have chosen to have a dog as part of your life, it has to be a two way street for you both to benefit from the relationship. It hardly seems fair to bring a dog into your home and then leave her at home every day, while you go about your daily routines and work and not expect a reaction from her. Enjoy your dog, and enjoy your journey together towards having the perfect family pet.

18 Dedication

This book is dedicated to all the dogs that I have had the privilege to get to know, who became less lonely because their owners took the time to understand them and get them help.

For further Dog Training Information, you can find me on:

Facebook
- Julie Hindle
- Ace Canine
- Tibetan Terrier Training and Behaviour Workshop
- Tibetan Terrier Grooming and Health Workshop
- Abelenus Tibetan Terriers
- Dog Training, Behaviour and Care Books I have written

Amazon
- Pre-Vaccination Puppy Training
- It's Okay to be Alone
- Clever Canine: Intelligent Training for Dogs (August 2017)

Made in the USA
Middletown, DE
07 January 2019